How Bad

YOU

Want It?!

By

Rebecca T. Harris

How Bad Do YOU Want It?!

- *Your Goals*
- *Your Dreams*
- *Get It Done Your Way!*

For any athlete trying to reach their next level!

By

Rebecca T. Harris

Dedication

To every kid that still dreams in color and believes they can achieve anything, this is for you. To those that do not give up easily and are relentless in their pursuit to accomplish their goals, this is for you. For those that just need a little extra push and added motivation towards the things in their life that seem far out of reach or difficult, this is for you. To every little girl wondering if they should play, hoping they get an opportunity to run with the best of them, wanting to stand out instead of fitting in, this is for you. To every kid that's been picked last or wasn't picked at all, this is for you. I've had my ups and downs with this journey and have felt every bump in the road you could possibly imagine, but anything is possible when you really want it bad enough! For the believers, this book is for you!

CONTENTS

CHAPTER 18

CHAPTER 19

CHAPTER 1

Introduction

Hi, my name is Rebecca Harris, and I wrote this book to help guide and inspire student-athletes along their journey. I was once a student athlete myself, who went from playing basketball at a Junior College (JUCO) in the small town of Ina, Illinois, called Rend Lake College, to a Division I athlete at the University of Illinois, and then on to play professionally, which is what I currently still do. My journey wasn't easy, and there was even less information available when I was coming up. I had no idea where to turn when looking for answers, but I always had a plan and kept my ultimate goal in mind.

There were times when I had to take a road less traveled and didn't know where to get information, or even who to ask. There were even times when my ultimate goal of playing at the professional level seemed to be far-fetched to others, but I NEVER wavered. Nothing was guaranteed or for certain, but I was always ready to put in the work and accept the challenge.

Since graduating from the University of Illinois in 2008, I've played overseas professionally for over 10 seasons, and in several different countries. Those countries include Poland, Germany, Turkey, Greece, the Czech Republic, and most recently, the Ukraine. I also played in Euroleague competition as well. This has allowed me the opportunity to play against the best of the best and to travel the world. Throughout this time frame, during my off-seasons from playing abroad, I would spend my time training and working out with young athletes while also working for the United States Junior Nationals (USJN), learning plenty about the Amateur Athletic Union (AAU) circuits and the recruiting process.

In 2012 and again in 2016, I took breaks from playing to accept coaching opportunities at the high school and college levels. And to top it all off, I discovered the many other opportunities there were to play beyond college in the U.S. outside of the WNBA. I play with the St. Louis Surge during my off seasons from playing overseas and it's going on eight summers now. We have won 2 national titles and been the runner up 3 different times.

It is because of my personal experiences that I have decided to help guide others on their journey. If there is anything I can do to help, it is to provide some answers and insight into the many questions and missing parts I had along my journey. I have gone through the recruiting process twice as a student- athlete, once in high school and once more while at a JUCO. From having a plan for where I wanted the sport of basketball to take me overall, to the networking and making connections I have made with coaches and GMs worldwide, you will read about what I've been able to accomplish and all that I've seen from coaching and working with young student-athletes on many different levels.

I began writing this book a couple of years ago, while on the back of a bus. We were going to a hotel in the middle of Germany as we were heading to an away game. I had just responded to one of many Twitter DMs I get from high school student-athletes. She asked me how she could get to the next level and what were some of the things I did to make it all happen for me. The student-athlete reached out to me because they thought that I was still the head coach at Rend Lake College at first. Whether it is from different student-athletes across the nation, parents, friends, or other people who hoop, I am often asked questions or for advice on my personal experiences around the game. The most common question I receive is, "What can I do to get to the next level?"

At this point, when I look at all the opportunities I have had to be around the game, to play it, and to develop the ones coming up after me, I have truly been blessed. I have been able to experience that "next" level a few different times, and I often think about what I wish I knew while I was coming up. My experiences as a student-athlete were full of trial and error, simply because

I did not have any real guidance from anyone who had been through it already. But at the end of the day, I always knew what my ultimate goal was and that I was willing to do the work to make it happen.

Along the way, I discovered several different routes I could take in order to accomplish my goal, and nowadays, I go about life trying to be the individual I wish I had while I was coming up to help guide me through the process. I found myself asking the question, "How can I continue to help those that seek to know what I know now?" With over ten years of experience as a professional athlete, after transferring from a JUCO to a Division I university as a student-athlete, as a high school and college head coach, and having the opportunity to spend eight summers with USJN/Blue Star Basketball working the AAU circuit, I provide a unique view and perspective on the ins and outs of the process as a student-athlete.

At a young age, I decided I wanted to play at the next level, and from that point on, most of everything I did was geared towards making that happen. Was it easy? No. Was it worth it? Absolutely. My path took some twists and turns along the way, but I always kept my eye on the prize and kept my end goal in mind! If you are willing to do the same, you can achieve anything! There were times when side steps needed to be taken to get that big leap heading in the right direction. And when the dream seemed far-fetched

13

and out of reach, times arose where my decisions became tough to make because there were more options than I originally anticipated and could not see at first.

For the athlete that wants their shot to continue playing their sport at the next level, this is for you. For the athletes that are highly recruited, the athlete that doesn't think they're getting the offers they would like to see, or the athlete that just wants an opportunity to continue playing no matter where it comes from, this is for each, and every one of YOU! If you don't see some of the offers you would like to, not being recruited at all, wondering what it is you are or are NOT doing to get some type of notice from coaches at that next level that you seek? THIS IS FOR YOU!

This book will help guide you throughout your athletic journey and much more! I'm someone who has gone through the process in several different ways and has had the opportunity to experience it from several different angles. I am often asked questions about what athletes can do to reach their next level and what recruiters and coaches are looking for. If you have the drive and passion to continue playing, there is a coach out there looking for an athlete like you.

In this book, I will give you some insight into **HOW** to go about the process and give you tips to move things in your favor towards reaching that next level. This is not about telling you exactly what route you should take, but to get you to become more involved in the process so you can create your best set of opportunities. But not only is this a guide to get you to the next level in your sport's journey, this is also a way of life that will help you find new ways and a discipline towards reaching all the goals you hope to achieve. So often, people quit pursuing certain goals because they get discouraged along the way due to having a set of expectations for themselves without realizing some steps that need to take place before hand.

Every journey throughout this process is NOT and will NOT be the same, but your journey will be unique and what you make of it. It may not come easy, but it can still happen. But ONLY if you are willing to put in the WORK! You can do this, you can make this happen, but you will need to ask yourself one fundamental question first...

"HOW BAD DO YOU WANT IT?"

Understand that getting a scholarship or playing a sport in college is not easy by any means. I know some athletes out there have made it look easy, but trust me, it is not. It takes a level of commitment and mental toughness that not everyone has, nor are they ready to tap into. At times, it takes a combination of a lot of hard work with a little bit of luck. But you know what they say, "if it were easy, everyone would be doing it." If this is something that you really want to do, then let's talk about some things that can help you make this a reality and get you to *YOUR* next level.

Things didn't always go according to plan, everyone didn't always have the answers I was seeking, or they didn't have MY best interest at heart. With my goal always in mind, I accomplished much more than I originally planned because I pivoted and side-stepped when I needed to. And even to this day, I'm still doing just that to reach MY next level! From the many coaches and players that I've either competed with, for, or against, and athletes I encountered worldwide, and the significant number of connections I made through sports, I have gained a wealth of knowledge. It's not just the ins and outs of the entire process but also the different ways of navigating my way through it all to accomplish the overall goal. Knowing how to play the game within the game is more than half the battle. There are so many things coaches look for in their athletes, and there are several different routes an athlete can take to get to where they want to go.

If there's one person I wish I had during my time as a high school student-athlete, it would be a professional athlete or even a college athlete to take me under their wing. I needed someone to tell me all the little things that people, usually people like yourself, have always had to find out on their own through trial and error. Many people talk about how bad they want to make their dreams a reality, but rarely are they willing to put in the work and effort it might take to make these things happen.

When they realize that it might take a lot more sacrifice than what they initially thought, sometimes they let that dream die. Or they then realize it wasn't a real dream of theirs to begin with. Especially if they let it slip away so easily once things began to get tough. But when you have a dream so big and ultimately a goal you really want to achieve, you do the work it takes to accomplish it. You take the bumps in the road and the lumps along the way. You do all you can to find the answers you need to prepare yourself for when an opportunity arises, and you map out the routes you can take to get there. You ultimately take ownership of every piece regarding your journey.

Now, I'm not saying this to try and discourage you from going after all the things you want. Quite the contrary, I hope you will take this as a challenge and a guide, a way to help you prepare for the road ahead. And not just on this pursuit of your next level in athletics, but to help you reach ALL of your dreams and goals that you plan to accomplish throughout your lifetime. This is a stepping stone, along with a blueprint to help you navigate throughout this journey.

My mission is to help and give guidance, and to provide more insight and knowledge than I had throughout my process as a student-athlete. To share with you a few of the "secrets" that no one ever tells you along the way. May you never let anything stand in your way while you accomplish your goals.

"Success is the sum of small efforts, repeated day in and day out." – Robert Collie

Now... let's get started!

CHAPTER 2

Make The Decision

First off, the sooner YOU know, the better! I understand that this part can seem easier said than done, but it can also be really simple. If your dream is to play at the next level, then begin speaking it into existence as early as possible. It does not matter how old you are, how tall you are, or where you live. What matters most is whether or not you are willing to put in the work to chase your dreams. The earlier you decide what it is you want to do, or the earlier you at least know what it is you want to go after, the more time you allow yourself to make that a real possibility! It's up to you and ONLY you to make the decision.

There are two very important questions that every athlete should ask themselves when going on this journey:

1. *How bad do I want to make it to the next level?*

2. *What is my ultimate goal? (The DREAM of all dreams if you could accomplish ANYTHING in this world.)*

"Are the habits you have today on par with the dreams you have for tomorrow...Your future is what you design it to be."

— Alan Stein Jr.

How bad do YOU want to make it to the next level?

Now, I seriously want you to take some time to think about this. How bad do **YOU** want it? How bad do you want to make it to the next level? Do you envision yourself playing at the varsity level, collegiate level, or even professional level? Are you willing to fight for this dream of yours? Or is this "dream" something that everyone else around you tells you that you're good at? Do you know the reasons behind WHY you want to make it to your next level? These are all questions that you should be asking yourself.

As you were coming up, maybe you have had people in your corner pushing you and encouraging you to continue to play, but this is not about them because they are not the one playing and pushing their mind and body to the limit. Sometimes people do things because they don't want to let anyone down, or because they are unsure of the actual path they want to take in life. Is this you? Can you relate? These questions are all about you and what you sincerely want for yourself in the end. Although we are mainly speaking on your athletic

21

journey, understand that knowing WHY you are choosing this path of athletics is important. The answer will also help you understand the length of time you will need to dedicate to reach your goal.

Once again, is this something that YOU really want for yourself, and is this something you really want to accomplish? Or is this something other people think you should do because of your talent or size, perhaps? And why? Think about that for a moment, I'm not asking your friends, not Mom and Dad, not the neighborhood, not everyone that has always told you that you were "great." The decision is about YOU and ONLY YOU. Have you actually taken the time to sit and think about why you play the sport you play and what it would mean for you to reach the next level? THIS is the first thing you need to do, evaluate how bad you want this and your reasons as to why you want it.

There are many different reasons behind why people pursue certain goals, and everyone's reasons can be different. Make sure you realize and recognize yours, and you'll become unstoppable in your pursuit!

Have you ever just taken the time to sit down and think about your "why?" If you haven't before, now is the time to do so. Identifying your "why" is a part of the journey and allows you to understand what it is you are working so hard towards and the different routes you can take to make it happen.

Allow me to share my top 5 reasons for making it to the next level coming out of high school.

1. *Get a degree and get my education paid for.*

- I took it as a great accomplishment to go from high school to college and get a degree within four years. No one in my immediate family had a degree at the time, so I would be the first to take that route.

2. *Attend a big university and represent them on and off the court. (UNC was my dream school at the time.)*

- Growing up on the other side of the world and living abroad most of my life, the only colleges and universities I knew about were the big named Division I schools. I had always dreamed of playing on the big stage, hopefully making it to the "big dance" during March Madness and winning it all with my squad! Rocking the team colors and representing the name across my chest was always a dream of mine.

3. *Prove people wrong about my abilities on the court and play at the highest level.*

- As a female athlete playing this game, the amount of people who helped put that chip on my shoulder when it came to proving others wrong is pretty long. From college coaches at various levels who said I wouldn't make it (mainly because I let them know I would be choosing a different direction other than their program), opponents from other schools, to the boy that gave me a black eye when I was 9 yrs. old because I crossed him up in front of his friends. Many of these situations were in the back of my mind while pushing towards making it to the next level. They helped motivate me.

4. *Accomplish a big step towards making it to the*

*professional level. (**ULTIMATE GOAL**)*

- Knowing that I wanted to become a professional athlete, from everything that I had seen about female professional basketball players who were American, they all had one thing in common, and that was playing college basketball first. More specifically playing at the Division I level before going on to play professionally.

5. *Travel*

- I love traveling to new and exciting places! I love exploring other areas, and it was important to choose an opportunity that would allow me to travel a bit, be far enough away from home to be comfortable, and give me a change of scenery.

Now that I have shared with you my top 5 reasons for wanting to get to the next level out of high school, I want you to go ahead and list 5 reasons WHY you want to make it to the next level. These reasons can literally be anything and everything. To make it to the next level, you need to understand the things you value most and what you hope to get out of your own experience.

Top 5 Reasons

_____

_____

_____

_____

_____

_____

_____

_____

_____

_____

_____

_____

_____

_____

_____

_____

_____

_____

_____

_____

_____

_____

_____

What is my ULTIMATE goal?

Everyone's answer to this question won't necessarily be the same, and that is perfectly fine because it shouldn't be. People play sports for a variety of different reasons. The answer(s) to this question should be in line with the top 5 reasons you gave for wanting to play at the next level. But for you, what is your ultimate goal and dream behind making all this happen in the first place? Your ultimate goal is the reason behind all of your hard work and why you want this so bad. What would you like to accomplish in the long run that would make you feel like you did all of this and came out a success in the end? What goal will push you day in and day out, no matter what else is happening in your life? Your ultimate goal is equivalent to the pot of gold at the end of the rainbow. Therefore, it is imperative that you know what drives you along this journey. After deciding to go on this athletic journey, knowing your reasons WHY and the ultimate goal that you are trying to accomplish will push you to do all the things that many refuse to do to make it. This will help you go that extra mile.

Listed below are some examples of "ultimate goals" that some athletes try to pursue through their journey with sports:

- For some, the dream is to make it to the big leagues (NBA, WNBA, NFL, NHL, NBL) or to play professionally at any level where they get paid.

- Maybe you want to make it to the Division I level in athletics or any level at all beyond high school.
- You could have the goal of becoming a part of a specific team or conference. (Have you ever seen the movie Rudy?[1])
- Some people want the opportunity to make a lot of money by playing at the professional level. There is a real financial goal attached to their dream and the success they hope to achieve through "making it" in sports.
- Others just want the opportunity to earn a scholarship that will cover their education, and then they have no plans of playing beyond that.
- There are those that look at sports as their only option of having a better life coming from the life that their families have been living.
- You may decide to enter into the world of sports at the college level as an athlete to hopefully later become part of the business side of things. (Ex: Going from player to grad assistant and moving up the ladder to full-time coach).

[1] The movie Rudy, is about a young man named Rudy Ruettiger (Sean Astin) who wants to play football at the University of Notre Dame, but has neither the money for tuition nor the grades to qualify for a scholarship. Rudy redoubles his efforts to get out of the steel mill where his father works when his best friend (Christopher Reed) dies in an accident there. Overcoming his dyslexia thanks to his friend and tutor, D-Bob (Jon Favreau), Rudy gains admission to Notre Dame and begins to fight his way onto the school's fabled football team.

And just so we are clear, these are just a few of the many reasons people choose to pursue their next level in sports. Also, these things do not necessarily coincide with one another. It is possible to play professionally and not have played at the highest level like the WNBA or NBA for basketball. You could also make it to the professional level and NOT make $1 million in the end. Trust me, I know! You can also earn a scholarship to play at the next level of collegiate sports, graduate with the type of degree you want, and not attend a Division I school.

If you know what your ultimate goal is in the end and follow along with this guide, you will see that there are several ways to accomplish your goal and you will accomplish much more along the way. It will become easier to starve your distractions and to continue pushing forward. There are so many misconceptions that come along with playing at the collegiate and professional levels. Everyone has their own story, journey, and path, which makes each student-athlete different and unique. Embracing the many different ways one can use to get to their next level, and putting in the effort to make it happen will make you unique, set you apart, and give you the opportunity you have been seeking. Getting to your next level will make every part of the journey well worth it!

Knowing what you want to do and accomplish by reaching the next level will help you narrow down some ways to go about your journey. The more you know, and the more information you have, the better off you will be going into this process and making decisions towards accomplishing your goals! In the end, it is always good to know what your ultimate goals and dreams are and to know what you are striving for. When you keep your eye on the prize and stay motivated towards accomplishing your goals, you are guaranteed to do some great things along the way. This is your journey, embrace it. Have a vision for your ultimate goal and allow it to create the purpose for your journey.

"Without dreams and goals there is no living, only merely existing, and that is not why we are here."

– Mark Twain

What are your ultimate goals and dreams that you hope to achieve?

_____

_____

_____

_____

_____

_____

_____

_____

_____

_____

_____

_____

_____

_____

_____

_____

_____

_____

_____

_____

_____

Now that you have written out your goals and some of the things you hope to accomplish, this should help drive you and motivate you to keep going. Look at them every day and often! Be motivated by your own words! Each one of your lists holds the keys to **WHY** you are doing what you are doing and **WHERE** you are trying to go! Use them continuously to push yourself in your journey towards success. Always remember your WHY; that way, when times get tough and when you feel like giving up, and you have doubts about the sacrifices you are making, your WHY is there for that extra push! This is your way of knowing and understanding why you are sacrificing certain things to get to where you are trying to go on your journey.

CHAPTER 3

What Are You Willing To Sacrifice?

Sacrifice – What Are You Willing To Do And Change?

"Goal setting is not only about choosing the rewards you want to enjoy, but also the costs you are willing to pay."

– James Clear

This is the question that seriously separates you from the rest of the pack. What are you willing to sacrifice and give up to accomplish your goals? You might even be thinking that right now you have been sacrificing plenty already. Or that it will be very easy for you to sacrifice even more when the time comes. You need to understand that with each new level of growth, with each road less traveled, there lies plenty of sacrifice!

What are you willing to give up? Will it be time with friends and family? Will you give up some of your favorite foods and change your diet? Will it be the time you spend playing video games, going to the mall with friends, or sleeping in bed allday?

Really take a moment and think about this! Athletes who are serious about getting better and about reaching their next level make plenty of sacrifices. It is no one's responsibility but your own as the athlete to see your goals through. Do not put it on Mom and Dad to make sure you're up on time for school or practice, do not put it on them to make sure your uniform is washed and ready for practices and games, and do not put it on them to have your equipment ready and schedules organized. These are all your responsibility and no one else's. An athlete who is serious about their dreams and these things will take the initiative and show ownership of their duties. They will make sure their alarms are set because they don't want to miss school or practice, it means too much to them. They will make sure their uniforms are clean and their equipment is ready to go because they want to be sure they are prepared for practices and games.

During my summers as a high school athlete, I would spend nearly every day at the gym or a park. Usually, twice a week, I would go 2-3 times a day to work out and be on the court. My friends never questioned our relationship when they didn't see me for days or weeks at a time. Most of my friends would hit the gym a time or two as well. I made sure to surround myself with those that understood me and knew where my priorities were because of where I was heading in my life. The right ones in your corner will always understand.

There were times where I sacrificed dates,

trips, parties, and time within certain social groups among my peers, but it worked out, and that's all I can ask for. Looking back, as a young teenage girl, I wish I had participated in some things here and there. But I made sacrifices to reach my ultimate goal, and to this day, most people who respected my decision are still in my life now.

These things and actions are the difference makers when it comes to being an "interested" player or a player who is "committed" and willing to make real sacrifices to achieve their goals. During the actual season, it's "easy" to put in the work. Your schedule is set, and there are others (your teammates) working right next to you. These are the perfect circumstances for those that are "interested." But it's during the summer or unprecedented times (no one could have prepared for something like Covid-19) when those deeply "committed" and willing to sacrifice really show up! Think about how you use your offseason. When do you sacrifice the most?

"God doesn't take things away to be cruel. He takes things away to make room for other things. He takes things away to lighten us. He takes things away so we can fly."

– Pat Summitt

Now, make your list.

What Are You Willing To Sacrifice?

_____

_____

_____

_____

_____

_____

_____

_____

_____

_____

_____

_____

_____

_____

_____

_____

_____

_____

_____

_____

_____

_____

_____

_____

CHAPTER 4

What Do You Want To Gain Out Of Your Athletic Career?

Your Ultimate Goal

"If you don't know what you want to do, then someone will always be able to tell you what you should do."

-Rebecca T. Harris

I have always lived and stood by this quote. Knowing where I wanted my athletic career to take me fueled almost every decision I made along the way. There were times when people would try and pull me in one direction or another, but if it wasn't in line with my ultimate goal or something to move me closer to it, I was not all that interested. Even though I didn't have all the answers while I was coming up, I had an idea of what things needed to look like to make it to the next level. I had an idea of the bigger picture. Doing my own research, allowed me to follow the footsteps of those I thought were good influences and on a similar path. Plus, the movie "Love and Basketball" had just come out, and I became even more obsessed with the game. And if I may say so myself, that movie paints a good enough picture of what life was like for a black female basketball player growing up only wanting to be the best ball player she could be, all while navigating high school.

Things are slightly different now, with a lot more opportunities than when I was younger. But to accomplish my ultimate goal and become a professional athlete, I knew that my best chances to achieve that would be to make sure I played at the highest level for college basketball, which was Division I. Why was this the route that I felt was a must for me to take? When paying attention to both the NBA and WNBA Draft, from about 1998-2004, I only saw players that played Division I get selected for the most part. This was especially true for the WNBA. With that in mind, I went about the process by telling myself that to give myself the best chances, Division I was the level I needed. Throughout high school, playing Division I became a huge focus of mine, but as you will later see in this book, I had to take a side step because I did not take care of everything I was supposed to along the way.

Whenever I would receive recruiting letters from

college coaches and universities, I would separate them by division. After that, I would look up each team, their coaching staff, and the type of schedule they played. I was looking for teams that had players that were drafted or played against several teams from which players had been drafted. Knowing what I was looking for within my journey helped me weed out a lot of the jargon that some coaches may try and use to sell their program. Not saying I didn't give everyone a chance or at least listen to a "sales pitch." There were just things that were non-negotiable because they did not fit into my overall vision, which included another level of basketball after college. I ultimately wanted to make it to the professional level, but there were other things I had plans of accomplishing along the way as well. And as long as YOU know your non-negotiables, that's all that matters. You don't even have to discuss them.

Coming into my senior year of high school, I was slated to go Division I; but I had to alter my original plan and take a different route. This was partially due to my grades but primarily due to my vision for myself. I had been highly recruited by quite a few schools and different conferences throughout my first 3 years of high school, but I did not see the schools I had pictured myself being a part of during the recruiting process. I had my goals, values, and the things I was looking forward to getting out of my college and athletic experience at the forefront of my mind, and none of those schools matched up for me at first.

Finishing up my senior year of high school, I

knew I would want a coach and program that would push me physically and mentally, I wanted to compete and win games, not just be a part of a program and along for the ride. This was a necessity for me and I couldn't settle for just anything because I also wanted the best opportunity to get me to the next level beyond college. Not only that, since my side-step required me to take a new route, which included going to a JUCO first, I had to change up my research and figure out which program would best suit me towards making that leap to the Division I level afterwards. As I went on several visits to JUCOs across the Midwest, a few factors that I knew I needed to focus on to be successful at this stage were to 1.) be relatively close to home 2.) make sure that the gym would be available pretty much whenever I wanted to get workouts in, and 3.) that the library would be open until a decent hour.

Now let me tell you why these things were essential for me during this stage of my journey. Being relatively close to home for me was a necessity because I wanted to have the ability to hit the gym back home as often as possible. The group of guys that I would work out with from my sophomore year of high school to my sophomore year of college were vital in my journey to making the leaps to each new level of basketball. Also, I wanted to be far enough away to feel like I had moved out of the area and was on my own a little, but close enough so that my family could come watch games and if something happened, they could get to me because I would not have a car my first semester. As a certified gym rat, I was looking for a school that would provide me with access to the gym when I would most likely want to be in there and get in some extra work. And at this point in my life, I had not encountered many teammates or female athletes like myself who would spend a lot of their free time in the gym. I wanted to make sure that when I wanted to stay late after practice, come back in later, or come in early, it would be open. During my recruiting process, I found that everyone didn't go about opening their gym the same, so I took note of that.

And lastly, I needed a library that would be open late. You see, I was on a mission like no other. If I wasn't in practice, getting in more work on the court or in class, I planned to be hitting the books and in the library. I wanted to give myself the best chances of making it to a top university to play ball, but to also get an excellent education in the long run. Being at the JUCO level was just the beginning.

My mindset after graduating high school was that I was now officially an adult, and I needed to take care of business all-around, in ways that I did not do before. Making sure that I excelled in the classroom was a huge part of that thought process; in high school, my grades were subpar, but I knew they needed to be better, and I needed to be better. It's up to you to put in the work to accomplish your hopes, dreams, and aspirations towards your ultimate goal. If you are willing to work hard, then great things will ultimately take place!

NOW
LET'S
GO
TO
WORK!

CHAPTER 5

Do Your Research

Your next step is crucial. Think about it, why wouldn't you want to know as much as possible about a place and environment that could potentially help you reach your ultimate goal? The location you choose has the potential to be where you will dedicate a lot of your time. This will also be a place, a team, and a school that will be considered a significant part of your life and a stepping stone towards where you would like to end up in the long run. You should want to know as much information as possible about this place, the school, the area, and the people you could potentially be surrounded by for the next 1-4 years.

By doing some research beforehand, you will figure out the questions you will need answers to throughout this process. Gather the information to help you know whether or not a school or that environment will be the right fit for you. It will at the very least let you know how much time you will need to dedicate to the institution before needing to take a leap or sidestep in a different direction. Before you began to dive into this book, one of the first things I mentioned was "the sooner you know, then the better." If you know or at least have an idea about what you want your ultimate goal to be as a freshman or sophomore in high school, this will give you more time to research and find answers that would be quite helpful along your journey. You might even know what your ultimate goal is before reaching high school; I know I did.

For example, if your ultimate goal is to get your education paid for, you may be more open to receiving a scholarship from almost ANY institution because they will pay for school and give you the opportunity to continue playing. But if your ultimate goal is to go to medical school, and get that paid for through an athletic scholarship, you would be more interested in trying to play at the highest level you can to gain access to some of the best medical schools in the nation. But do you even know which schools those are or where they are located? RESEARCH!!

Here are some questions to ask yourself while entering the beginning stages of your research:

1. What are the schools in my area?

Coaches are always looking for local talent. And although it does get overlooked at times, if you take that initiative on your own, you might just be creating your very own opportunity. If you are looking to get your first opportunity and you have not been recruited thus far, it's best to get to know the programs within your area.

2. What division of athletics are these schools?

Knowing and understanding the different divisions for the programs around you will benefit you based on your ultimate goal. Various programs and divisions can offer different types of scholarships. Depending on the coach and the program's history, their networks and reach will also be different.

3. Do these schools offer the major I am interested in?

If you already know the major you hope to study, why settle for an institution that cannot give you what you seek? Have your non-negotiables, the things you are not willing to sacrifice, at the forefront of your mind while answering this question. That will help you narrow your search tremendously.

4. Who are the coaches for my sport at these schools?

Find out who the coaches are and begin building relationships. Ask your coaches to reach out to them as well and see what they are looking for in incoming recruits. Get an understanding of the type of program they run and who they may have coached in the past.

5. How have the teams for these schools performed in the last few years? Their record?

Understanding a little bit about where a team has been will help you know where the team is trying to go. If they had a losing season, what can you offer to try and turn things around? Do you see yourself as a good fit for their program? If you have an ultimate goal of playing as a professional, does this team have any notable opponents on their schedule? Did any former players make it to the professional level?

6. Who will be graduating and leaving the team by the time I get there?

Without knowing who the coaches are currently recruiting, you will at least see what positions will need to be filled on that roster for the upcoming season. Whether you are highly recruited or not, this is information that you should find out for yourself. If making it to the next level is truly something you want to accomplish, and it is a dream of yours, do not solely rely on other people and coaches to make it happen for you.

Seek out the results you want. Start by doing

49

your research because you might find that the opportunity you are looking for has been within arm's reach this entire time. Within an hour or two from many locations, there are possibly some schools with which you are not familiar. Most student-athletes remain fixated on a "big name" school or the top division right away, and that's all they think about. Just remember, there are several ways to accomplish the same dream.

There are plenty of schools of different sizes and different divisions that could help you along your journey. If you continue to keep your end goal in mind, you'll figure out what schools fit you and can help you reach and accomplish your ultimate goal. Most people miss out on either a great first opportunity or THEIR perfect opportunity because they do not consider all options and possibilities in the beginning. There are plenty of smaller schools that are always looking for athletes and students to attend their programs. It's best if you get to know schools in all divisions (D1, D2, D3, NAIA, & JUCO, to name a few) and within your area first.

For the highly recruited athlete, athletes with a few offers, or the athlete that is preparing to be highly recruited in the future, take note of this:

A coach's job is to sell their school and their program to you as the recruit first and foremost. They have a job to do as a coach, and that is to bring in players.

Things might look like heaven on Earth to you, especially if you don't have an accurate idea of what it is you want out of your athletic journey or collegiate experience. Here is why doing your research is so important. Any athlete that's ever gone on an "official visit" can tell you, the red carpet is rolled out to make it seem like this school is the perfect fit for you. So they will show you all of the things they know you want to see and put bright lights in front of them while not really showing you the less flattering things. But if you already know a bit about what you are looking for, you won't get blinded and sidetracked by the glitz and glamour, although that treatment can be pretty exciting.

Another reason it's essential to do your research is because there are SO MANY misconceptions out there about the different levels of basketball and other sports. The main one is that "any athlete playing at a level other than Division I is NOT as good a player as those that are on the Division I level." And although there are certainly cases where that is true, that's just not always the case, and it's a blanket stereotype. People choose schools and athletic programs for many different reasons.

Different athletes are presented with various opportunities at other times. You NEED to do research for yourself and create your own opportunities! Knowing what your ultimate goal is and what you are working towards accomplishing will only help you to make the best decisions for you and your future.

Do not get sidetracked and caught up in the opportunities that other athletes may have had or are getting around you. Focus on where you are trying to get to at the end of your journey, and take notes along the way. All levels can play and have some of the most talented athletes. All levels provide you with a degree. All levels have players that have been known to become professionals down the road. But the questions you'll need answers to are;

"Do these schools in particular, have the degree that I want?"

"Is there a style of play or a coach where I think I would be a perfect fit?"

"What programs have the most players to go on and play at the professional level?"

"Which programs will give me the best chances to continue my career?"

"How is their overall network and connections with other coaches and possible agents?"

"Which programs have full-ride scholarships and which have partial scholarships to offer?"

These are questions to ask yourself and help you figure out which programs will best suit you along your journey.

When I was in middle school, I knew that I wanted to take basketball as far as it could take me. Actually, I wanted to become the first female basketball player to enter the NBA. This was all before the WNBA came about, but when the WNBA came around in 1996, I was even more excited about the possibilities because there was a league now specific to women at the highest level for basketball! At the time, I was living overseas as a military brat and wasn't exposed to many female basketball players overall. My father was aware that I was talented and loved the game, so with any opportunity he found to have me around basketball, he tried his best to make sure I was a part of it.

Growing up, he was a well-respected basketball official and served in the United States Air Force. When we were stationed in the Philippines, Japan, and Germany, he allowed me to travel with him when he had games to officiate. I would be that little kid shooting at halftime and in between games. With that being said, my father made it a point to make sure we would be stationed in the United States by the time I would be entering high school to give me a better opportunity of being seen. In 1998, when I was in the middle of 7th grade, my family moved from Sembach Air Force Base, Germany, to Scott Air Force Base, Illinois.

At this time I was basically a foreign exchange student in my own country. We only knew about the big-named schools, which were all Division I programs. And that was mainly due to living overseas and only being able to see certain programs play in big matchups with ranked teams or during March Madness. Other than that, there would be the occasional NBA game on, and they would speak about the professional players and what schools they came from. That's how my dream school became the University of North Carolina; I was a huge Michael Jordan fan.

The whole process of getting recruited was completely new and foreign to us, so we learned everything we could on the fly. No one in my family had ever been through this process, and being new to living in the States at the time, to receive the best information, we weren't exactly sure who we could ask. I learned about a couple of small schools here and there throughout high school simply because of their location in comparison to where we lived.

Moving to Scott Air Force Base in Illinois, we were about 20 minutes from 2 small schools. Southwestern Illinois College, a Junior College, was also known as Belleville Area College when we first moved there. And then there was McKendree College (now McKendree University), which is an NAIA school. Honestly, if these schools weren't so close to me, I wouldn't have known much about them at all. They just weren't on my radar, and I didn't pay them much attention.

Had I done some actual research on my own, I would have realized that several other schools were within an hour of where I lived. That list includes Southern Illinois University-Edwardsville (DI), Saint Louis University (DI), Harris-Stowe University (DIII), Webster University (DII), Rend Lake College (JUCO), Kaskaskia College (JUCO), Greenville College (DIII), and that's just to name a few. Doing your research early could significantly expand your search and grant you more options.

Make a list of schools that are within 2 hours of you.

_____

_____

_____

_____

_____

_____

_____

_____

_____

_____

_____

_____

_____

_____

_____

_____

_____

_____

_____

_____

_____

_____

_____

_____

If you know what major you would like to
study, find out which of those schools on our
list offer that program or major.

_____

_____

_____

_____

_____

_____

_____

_____

_____

_____

_____

_____

_____

_____

_____

_____

_____

_____

_____

_____

_____

CHAPTER 6

Be Active On and Off The Court

"You can't control who's more naturally gifted than you, but you're in complete control of who you allow to outwork you."

– Coach Adam Hood (UTSA Assistant Men's Basketball Coach)

Doing the work on and off the court and going above and beyond will always go a long way. There are coaches all over the world who would rather have a hard-nosed athlete who gives more than they are asked to, over the lazy but talented athlete any day. Those types of players bring added value to any team they are on. If you are trying to get to the next level, start doing the hard work early.

A mistake that many young athletes make is

not being active enough in their pursuit of getting to the next level. Remember, this is your goal and no one else's. It goes for any athlete; whether you are highly recruited or not, take an active role in your journey. Often, athletes sit back and wait to be recruited, to receive a "sign," to be told when to get a workout in. They wait for a coach to approach them instead of taking that step and introducing themselves to coaches first.

The recruiting process does not always happen the way you think it will or should, but when it is your ultimate goal to make it to the next level, why would you want to leave it solely up to chance? What if a coach never comes knocking? Then does that mean you give up? Do not get stuck waiting; take some initiative and take those first steps. Don't be afraid to get the ball rolling and start putting yourself out there! We're talking about your goals here, now how bad do you want it??

There are so many ways you can be active in your pursuit of playing at the next level. In this chapter, we will address three key ways that often are overlooked and very underrated. Any and every interaction involving people connected to that next level you are trying to reach, can help you. So whatever you can do to put yourself in those environments and in front of those individuals over the years, HELPS! Did you notice I said "individuals?" Remember, you never know who is watching and who has just the right connection that could work to your benefit.

5 Key Ways of Being Active In Your Pursuit

1. Try to attend a few sports camps at a few schools over the years.

I understand that sometimes college sports camps can be a bit on the pricey side, so maybe they are out of your budget. However, I am NOT saying you need to do this every week, of every summer, of every year. But, *if you know what you want to do* sooner, this can help. Going to a camp at a school you have some hopes of possibly playing for and attending puts you in front of these coaches EARLY. If you've done your research on who the coaches are and know the type of team and school you're looking for, this should narrow that search. And if you make a decent impression, this can lay the foundation for your quest to receive a scholarship or play at the college level later.

Now, notice I said a "decent" impression! And I say this because it's not always your skills that get you seen. It could be your character, your commitment to getting better, how you treated the other campers, or maybe how you spoke and approached the coaches! When you attend a camp, so many things can work in your favor, keep this in mind! Take advantage of being in front of the coaches and in that environment. Do more than just go through drills and be in attendance.

Being in this environment usually allows you the opportunity to meet and greet the players at this school and they are who you ultimately aspire to be like or even replace. It is a perfect time to pick

60

their brains and flood them with plenty of questions. Ask them about what worked and didn't work for them during their time in high school. Get to know things about the work they put in to get noticed by coaches and what to expect when playing at the next level. You may end up landing the perfect relationship that helps you get another inside look at what it's like at the next level, along with someone willing to vouch for you with their coach!

2. Game Film – Make Sure You Have Some Film, And If You Don't Have Any, CREATE SOME!

I cannot tell you how many stories I've heard from former players at the high school and even college level, who were trying to make it further in their career, and say that their journey stopped because no one ever sent off their game film. Now, although I know everyone's circumstances are not the same, my first thought is usually, "what were YOU doing about your film, outside of what your coach was or wasn't doing?"

Remember, this is YOUR goal, your journey, and no one else's, so don't leave it up to chance or in anyone else's hands. If you are in a position where you feel like your game film is not getting sent out to coaches and is not available to them upon request, be sure to take these matters into your own hands. Consider ways of getting games filmed before the season even begins. These days having great snippets and certain types of plays captured on film can go a long way.

Here are a few ways to make sure you have some game film when the time comes:

1. Have your friends and family record pieces of the game if they can't record the whole thing.
2. Ask your coach for all the links to the games and the film itself, that way you'll have it to send out later on your own.
3. If you cannot get the film from your team or coach, ask the opposing team or coach for their recording or link of the game.

And I know some of these suggestions might seem "unconventional" to you, but honestly, they're not. Plenty of athletes have gotten to the next level and received their opportunity by going above and beyond to make things happen for themselves. In the end it will always come down to one simple question, how bad do you want it? It's about networking and building relationships that will make the process A LOT easier and get you closer to accomplishing your ultimate goal and your next level.

Now let's say you're not currently playing high school basketball or on any AAU team, but you are still working out and trying to get scouted and recruited in hopes of reaching the next level. Your options with game film are not the same, but are you going to let the fact that you aren't on a current team deter you from your goals? GO OUT AND MAKE SOME! Create your own film.

Rarely done, but still effective at times, record a good open run session. Playing pick-up basketball with some college athletes that are home on break?

Record! Playing pick-up with some "old school" park legends who still got it? Record! Getting in a great workout with a player development trainer? RECORD!! To reach your next level and get that opportunity, you will need to be willing to do some things that most people are not. Especially when your situation is a bit different, like not being on a current team. By any means necessary, be willing to create ways to make things happen in your favor. It also means you need to be more aware of your approach to playing pick-up, working out, and the opportunities around you since this would essentially be an audition tape you are making.

Start playing pick-up with a different mentality, mindset, and pursuit by being more intentional. Obviously, you can't control everyone while playing pick-up, but this isn't about everyone else; focus on the things you would want a coach at the next level to notice about you. Take quality shots that showcase some of your skills, run the floor, play solid one on one defense, box out, and rebound. These are all things with little details that you can focus on that a coach at the next level would love to have from a new member of their team if you can put it all together.

If you are already playing on a high school team or at least an AAU team, you want to make sure to have a FULL game recorded to send off. You also want to make sure this is one of, if not your BEST games possible. This game film should show many of the things you do well on the court and on both sides of the ball. On top of having a complete game recorded, it's a good idea to have a few highlight videos available as well. It could be a tape full of highlights from the entire season, the first half of the season, or a few moments from your best games overall. Within your highlight video, you should include great defensive and offensive plays.

Here are some things you will want to highlight and focus on within your game film:

For post players

- *Getting blocks*
- *Crashing the boards*
- *Grabbing rebounds*
- *Being in great defensive position*
- *Making it hard for the opponents to post up*
- *Making it hard for the offense to score*
- *Setting great screens*
- *Running rim to rim*
- *Calling for the ball*
- *Giving great outlet passes*
- *Making athletic plays around the rim*

For the guards and perimeter players

- *Handling the ball under pressure*
- *If you are a PG, setting up other players to score*
- *Knocking down open jump shots*
- *Getting to the basket*
- *Finishing in traffic at the rim*

- *Pushing the ball up the court*
- *Entry passes to the post*
- *Stopping your man from scoring*
- *Being in the right position defensively*
- *Using both hands to make passes*
- *Communicating and leading the team (PGs)*

Recap and tips of what to include in your highlight tapes

- *Make sure to include your most current contact information (Full name, email, current school, the color of your jersey, along with your jersey number)*
- *Be sure to put your best plays first*
- *Separate your offensive and defensive highlights*
- *Show yourself playing off the ball*

3. Attend games throughout the college season.

Any time you have an opportunity to attend a college game, no matter the division, you should go for it! Get to know the atmosphere and take it all in! If you really want to make it to the next level, seeing people in a position you hope to be in one day should inspire you in one way or another. Also, this helps with your research!

Watch how both teams play, how players and teammates interact with one another, and their coaches. Take note of the pace of the game and the different coaching styles being utilized. Attending a game allows you the opportunity to observe two programs at once. Can you see yourself playing for either program? Playing for either coach? Notice the things you like and love about a program, but also the things you're not so fond of. Could you see yourself working through the things you weren't so fond of viewing at the game? Take note of what players are doing and envision yourself in that same position. You should be able to walk away with a nice list of things that you could work on or even research to help your chances of getting to the next level.

Here are some thoughts and questions you should consider asking yourself while watching the game:

- *How are the players in your position playing?*
- *What are the differences in the level of their play vs. where you are now in yours?*
- *Can you see yourself playing for either program?*
- *Can you see yourself playing for either coach?*
- *What about the atmosphere in the gym did you like or dislike?*
    - » Size of the gym
    - » The overall facilities
    - » Fan base
    - » Amenities

4. Make contact and email coaches throughout the years.

If you have been doing your research, at this point, you should be able to at least put some faces to names with certain coaches at certain schools. Take the time and look them up if you haven't already!

Here are the steps to take that will usually lead you to some contact information for the coaches of the program you are looking into:

- *Look up the school online*
- *Go to their "athletics" page*
- *Find the tab or section that says "Sports"*
- *Find the sport you are interested in*
- *Then look for a tab for the "coaching staff."*

If you don't see a tab for the "coaching staff," then look for the tab "roster"

You should find an email address and a phone number attached to the names of each coach on the coaching staff. Sometimes you can find more information attached to their profiles that will provide you more ways to reach out to them, like their social media handles.

Referencing a previous section about doing your research, while you are on these web pages, look at things about the program, the institution, and the team. Get to know a bit about the school and their history. Also, there is usually a paragraph or a small bio to go along with a name and photograph attached to the coaches you are looking up. Use all of this information to your advantage in getting to know the coaches you want to reach out to and what questions you might want to ask when given the opportunity.

Once you have gotten some contact information, it's time to introduce yourself. Now, I'm NOT saying email them every day for the next five years. However, there is nothing wrong with a small introduction that tells a little about yourself, providing your stat line, an attachment with your best game and/or highlight, and your transcript.

Now that you have the contact information for the coach, SEND THEM AN EMAIL!!! Start reaching out! What are you waiting for? Not sure what to have in your email or how to start it? Here is a format example:

1. *Give a catchy subject – grab the coach's attention*
2. *Introduction – say "hello" and give basic details about yourself*
3. *Explain why you're interested in their program and your main reason for emailing*
4. *Make sure links and attachments are included*
5. *Conclusion – thank the coach for their time*

EMAIL EXAMPLE

Coach Box,

Good afternoon. I hope everything is going well. Great win against Illinois last week. Williams really went to work with a nice double-double to help seal the deal! I like the way she plays! I'm looking forward to watching the next game when you all play against Maryland.

My name is Rebecca Harris, and I'm a sophomore at Mascoutah High School in Mascoutah, Illinois. I just wanted to reach out to you and introduce myself. I know you are quite busy, so I appreciate you taking the time to read my email.

I love your program and hope to one-day play for you at that level. Attached below is one of my recent games and my transcript. Currently, I am a 5' 8" guard, averaging 12ppg 4stls 8rebs and 5asts. Whenever you have a moment, I would appreciate it if you could take a look at my game and give me a few pointers as to what I can work on to get better and be the player you are looking for!

Thank you so much for taking the time to read this! Good luck for the rest of the season, and I look forward to hearing back from you! Go Hoosiers!

Rebecca Harris

-Attached Link-

IMPORTANT MESSAGE FOR PARENTS

Allow your children to do this on their own. It's ok to check their spelling and grammar, but this is for them to do. It's all a process and a learning experience! With this email, they are already showcasing a bit of their personality and taking initiative when speaking to coaches. They are learning how to build a relationship and network, all while working towards accomplishing a goal of their own. This is exactly one of the things that coaches want to see from recruits, them taking the initiative and showcasing individuality and personality.

It is such an underrated and essential step, and more athletes should take the time and send an email to college coaches. The more you understand how this business and system works, the better. College coaches are just not able to see every recruit play in person, and there are several reasons why. First, there is the number of athletes trying to get to the next level, in comparison to the amount of coaches at these schools. Second, the amount of time, energy, and effort it takes to get around to see all the players. And lastly, trying to see these players in person, over time, during the allotted "recruiting periods." To work more in the athlete's favor, you, the athlete, need to try and make contact first, do not sit back and wait. College coaches often find recruits from recruits themselves, and emails are a great way to get on a coach's prospect list. By doing it this way, they can be intentional about trying to see you more vs.

going to see another athlete. If done right, you can go from having barely any coaches or no coaches at all recruiting you to being one of the hottest commodities overnight.

5. Fill out questionnaires

Something to also look for on college websites when looking for contact information is a tab or section that might have a questionnaire available for you to fill out. Any opportunity for you to fill out one of these, take it. Coaches will look at the traffic coming through on the website to see what athletes are interested in their program and who took the time to fill them out. And if a questionnaire is not on the website, that's fine. There are times where once an interaction between a player and coach begins, they may send a link to you to fill out a questionnaire later. It just allows them the opportunity to get more information about you, get to know you a little better, and to add you to their recruiting list and compare some things with other players.

CHAPTER 7

Networking + Creating Relationships = Opportunities

When trying to make it to the next level, it is important to make connections and build relationships along the way. For players who are actively playing on a select team or a high school team, what is your relationship with your current coach? Those coaches are already a part of your network and inner circle. Part of their job is to be an active source to get you to your next level and to help you successfully reach your goals. Your current coach can be a huge asset in your recruiting process, so you want to be sure to build a relationship with them throughout the season and throughout your time together.

Coaches at the next level will reach out to the coaches you have now, as well as your trainers and parents during the recruiting process. You would like the people in your inner circle to be aware of the goals you've set for yourself and for them to be able to speak highly on your behalf about your play,character, and work ethic. These are all people that are a big part of your network and can help during this process.

The number of players out there who have dreams and goals of reaching the next level but do NOT use the resources that are at their fingertips is astounding. Too many athletes sit back and wait for things to happen instead of taking some initiative and asking questions or making the first move, such as sending out emails to introduce themselves. This is a part of being active off the court in your pursuit, use your sources as much as possible. And that primary source, first and foremost, are the coaches you already have. Be sure to communicate your goals while also showing that you are working towards them, and it all starts with the team you are currently on. Coaches are more inclined to go above and beyond to help you when they see how much work you are putting in on your own! That means working hard in the classroom, during practices and games, and just goingthe extra mile to achieve your goals.

Here are some things to say to your current coach so that you are developing the type of relationship that helps you in the long run:

"Hey Coach, what are some things that I should work on to make it to the next level?"

Coaches have great respect for players that want to work hard and improve their game. They love the players that take the initiative and ask questions. The next time you and your coach are

74

having a conversation, ask them what areas of your game you could improve on. You will get an idea for what they would like you to work on for your current team, it builds an open line of communication, and it will also show your coach that you are trying to get better.

"Coach, is there anything else I can do to help our team?"

If you want to build a better relationship with your coach, ask them what else you can do to help your team. Have an open mind while asking this question because the team may need something that is not necessarily about things in practice or games. Coaches love players who are willing to sacrifice their personal aspirations and some of their time for the greater good, help a teammate or do some of the little things that makes the team better overall. It does not matter if you are considered the best or worst player on the team. Coaches love and appreciate this thought quite a bit!

"Coach, do you have time to watch game film and go over some things together?"

When athletes take the time to approach their coaches about watching film, this is the type of win-win most coaches LOVE! Not only does this show another way you are taking initiative, but also presents another opportunity for both of you to learn about one another. Everyone does not learn the game the same. The Coach may learn some things about you and your basketball IQ that they didn't know before and thus will further your relationship and the level of trust built. This act will help you see where you can improve your play on the court, but it also allows both of you the opportunity to talk about what you see and the different perspectives of the game.

"What do you think about____Coach?"

The key to building a better relationship with your coach is all about getting to know them and taking the time to ask questions. The more you ask questions and pick their brains, the better your relationship will be. You get to learn how they see the game and what they are looking for from their players. This will help you get to know them better as people, and it will build trust and respect between the two of you moving forward.

Communication is always key, but so is your timing. Ask these questions at a moment when your coach can break things down for you and give you their time. Whether you pull them aside, meet with them before or after practice, or respond to something said when your coach is not in the middle of a drill.

"If your coach has to constantly come to you and ask you to work hard, don't be surprised when you get replaced by someone who constantly comes to your coach asking for more work."

− Coach Matt Lisle via Twitter

Do not make the mistake of thinking that your talent and skill level are the only things that matter.

Another reason why building relationships and networking are so meaningful is that you never know what conversation will eventually lead to your opportunity. College coaches speak to other coaches as well, and whether you had a good or bad interaction with a coach, that information could travel. A college coach you may have personally had an encounter with, but may not have been right for you, or didn't have any scholarship opportunities for you at the time, may have easily sent your information as a referral to a friend of theirs who more than likely coaches in a different division or conference. That coach could have felt some great energy from you and thinks you deserve an opportunity, so he's networking on your behalf. This type of situation happens quite often, and as the athlete, you just never know who is looking out for you.

CHAPTER 8

School Visits

When you begin to get recruited by coaches, you are only allowed a certain number of "official" visits. These are visits that college coaches plan with and for you to show you around their campus and facilities, and basically roll out the red carpet for you in hopes of you choosing their program over others. However, you can make school visits regularly on your own. For the athlete not being recruited as much, or not at all, start taking school visits on your own. You could contact the institution and schedule a campus visit, that way someone at the school can show you around, take you on a tour, and introduce you to all the things that would be available to all the students that attend.

You should certainly take it upon yourself to visit the schools close to you. Check out the campus a bit, see what it looks like, and the things they can provide you as a student. If you do your research early enough, some campuses schedule "open house" tours before the school year begins, and you can join in on those that are already planned. You would walk around and look at the campus alongside a few other people who may be considering going to this school in the future. You would get more of an inside look into the student and campus life, rather than just the side of athletics.

This is another good reason to do your research as early as possible. Give yourself the opportunity to see some of the possibilities that are out there and to see what things fit you and the goals you have set for yourself. Make sure to take notes while keeping in mind your ultimate goal and the things you are looking for in a school as a student-athlete. During a school visit, take note of all the things you hope to see and have at an institution that you wish to attend.

Also, it is important to recognize and consider, all the things that you might not necessarily want to be around as well. These tours and visits should give you added motivation and help you to envision yourself attending an institution at the next level. Although most of your time would be dedicated to your studies and athletics, there are plenty of other things that take place on campus or its surrounding area that might make your experience at the next level that much more enjoyable and worthwhile. The whole point of doing your research and making campus visits is so you can get an idea of what will be available to you and how to make the most of your overall experience.

"Piggy-Backing" is also another option to consider when starting to visit schools. Let's say you have a friend or teammate who is being highly recruited, and they want you to come along on their "official visit." Now, you don't want to come along and hijack their visit, but you do want to take plenty of notes and see what that experience is like. Pay attention to everything that is going on, from the facility, surrounding area, school, and academics, to the players on their current roster. You should also pay attention to the current students attending the school and EVERYTHING that is being shown. Even take into account all of the things that are not shown to you, and ask yourself "why?"

Because this isn't your "official visit," the school can't treat you as the recruit in terms of paying for your expenses and travel, but the knowledge and experience gained from tagging along should be well worth it. Keep your ultimate goal in mind and have a few questions prepared before you go. Find the right moments to ask any questions about the school and team that might interest you, but before you take this visit with your friend, I would highly suggest that you MAKE SURE that it is ok for you to tag along AND for you to ask questions.

The right type of questions and energy could lead to this coach possibly adding you to their recruiting list or passing along your information to some other coaches they may know who are currently looking for players. It's important to understand that because a coach may have a

81

roster spot available, does not mean they also have a scholarship available. Being on this visit and having this opportunity to be in front of these coaches could even lead into offers for both you and your friend before you leave campus. I have seen it happen more often than not, and to those that genuinely deserved it after just asking the right questions.

CHAPTER 9

AAU Programs & Select Teams

Just like you are doing some research for a possibility and an opportunity to play at the next level, you should do some research on AAU programs and the select teams in your area as well. Playing on any select team is another option that can help you get in front of the right people, possibly boost your rankings across the nation, and get you noticed by college coaches. Even though playing AAU is not a must, it can be quite beneficial for you in the long run if you choose the right program fit. Find out what programs would best suit you and how they can help you get better as an athlete, and hopefully provide you with the right type of opportunities to further your athletic journey.

Don't know how or where to look for an AAU program?

Here are a few ways...

1. Be sure to ask around, ask your peers, teammates, and the high school coach. Word of mouth is usually the best- case scenario!
2. Google/Internet searches
3. Contact the rec centers and sports complexes near you and ask if they have any AAU tournaments on their schedule for the year. (They should be able to give you some contact information for the host of the tournament or some coaches who will be involved that can point you in the right direction.)
4. Social Media – Most teams have a social media presence. Search for their team Facebook page.

Things to look for within an AAU program...

1. Do they play in sanctioned events that college coaches attend?
2. What is their history as a program?
   a. Former athletes playing at the next level
   b. Do they play against other programs that have a history of getting players highly recruited?
   c. Are they known for developing their players?
3. Coaching staff
   a. Do the coaches have connections?

    b. Their success with player development and coaching

    c. Will they make you a better player and put you in situations to make you succeed?

4. Evaluate the talent of the current team
   a. Will your teammates push you to compete in practice?
   b. Will this team help you grow?

Things to consider when selecting an AAU team...

1. Will you actually have the opportunity to play?
2. Will the coaches be able to develop your skills and teach you more about the game?
3. Do the coaches have a network of college coaches to whom they can reach out to? Do they have connections?
4. Are the AAU coaches willing to make calls and send out game film on your behalf?
5. Does the program have a competitive playing schedule?
6. Cost and expenses
7. How knowledgeable are the coaches when it comes to the recruiting process as a whole?

Once you find a program, find out what types of tournaments they play in. There are NCAA sanctioned events that AAU teams can play in where college coaches attend and scout players. There are also tournaments that are held just so players can play more games and gain experience on the floor with better talent. And then there are tournaments that are put together for the sole purpose of someone trying to make money.

You will want to know which ones you are getting yourself into, so choose a team wisely. You can find these different types of tournaments across the nation. They are mainly held throughout the summer when college coaches are on their recruiting trails searching for talented players.

Something to also take into account is the fact that just because you make contact with the team and coach doesn't mean you'll automatically be on the team. Most of these teams hold tryouts, and then there are fees to be paid. Not only that, when and IF you do make the team, that doesn't necessarily mean you will get a certain amount of playing time. That is why it is crucial to do some research and make sure you get the right fit for you when it comes to an AAU program.

On another note, some tournaments and teams are run that allow you to just face off against different competition and test out some skills you have been working on and developing within your game. If you don't feel like you are ready for some of the more elite programs and tournaments, then look for those teams that will allow you to develop over the course of a summer or two before you step up your game and try to join one of the more elite and experienced AAU programs.

Before officially selecting the AAU program that you hope to be on, make sure that it will help you grow as a player more than anything. Choose a team that has the potential to assist you with getting to the next level by showcasing your skills on a different platform. Be sure to ask the AAU coaches about the players who have gone on to play at higher levels. You want to be able to reach out to people who have been in your same position. Playing AAU can be considered another level as well, so a lot of the questions and research you need to do to find what you are looking for are the same when choosing a college program.

Like I stated earlier, growing up, we had to learn things as we went along because we were new to living in the States and did not know much about anything regarding the recruiting process, let alone the AAU process. The first select team I became a part of, came together through a league I played in at the local sports complex. Most of these girls attended the same school, which was different from mine, and had known each other for quite some time.

A father of one of the players decided to form this team to provide an opportunity for his child and for the other girls she went to school with, whom he felt could take advantage of this new situation. They happened to know me from the league and invited me to join. That is how most of these select teams form. There was also some talk of me possibly going to their high school instead of the one I ended up attending, so I believe that may have played a small role in things. After all, we were still trying to figure everything out.

I spent about three seasons with this AAU team, but by the end of my Sophomore year in high school, it was time to move on and find another team that would keep pushing me to new heights. That decision was not the easiest. When you are young, constantly moving around, and finally feel like you have a constant group to be around, it can be tough when it's time to do some other things. But this move was necessary.

The next team I joined was run and coached by a friend of my Dad's that was also in the military. This team was a major upgrade talent-wise in the grand scheme of things. It had the top 1-2 players from every local high school in the area. We were stacked, and we knew it. It was fun, it was refreshing, and I made a whole new set of people with whom to compete with over the summer. Although we did have our run-ins during the actual high school season, this was much different. Everyone on this team ended up playing at the next level (Mizzou, Lipscomb, Indiana St, and SLU, just to name a few) except one who accepted a Track scholarship instead. Playing with this team definitely helped get me some looks that I was not getting before.

CHAPTER 10

Play Multiple Sports

These days, coaches have begun to appreciate athletes who play more than one sport a lot more than they used to. Let me tell you why! When you focus on more than one sport, your mind and body adjust to several different movements and conditions. You also have adapted the ability to read and react to different situations that you may not find in just one sport compared to the other. In addition to those things, this allows for versatility that can't necessarily be taught in one particular sport.

Here's what Travis Kelce of the Kansas City Chiefs had to say about playing multiple sports when he was younger from his interview on the All The Smoke Podcast:

"Growing up I played every single sport you could think of man. I was going from hockey practice, to basketball practice when I was in like 4th or 5th grade. I was playing baseball just about year round, hockey year round, soccer year round.

When it got to high school that's when I really had
to narrow it down........."

When asked if it was hard to change positions
in football to adapt to what was needed for Kelce
to be successful at the college level (and now pros)
going from QB to Tight End, this is what he had to
say...

"It was a complete change of mentality of
sitting in a pocket but I still had that same
physicality that I grew up with. Playing
hockey and lacrosse, and being the little
brother. Being able to take a hit, blindside
take a hit. Things like that, the traits were
easy to transition.

And then you take the ability to play on
the court. Be able to go up and grab a
rebound, be able to go up and grab an alley-
oop and take it off somebody's head. Things
like that, the athletic ability that transferred
from the court over, the ability to track a
baseball. The ability to go deep and run down
the sidelines and track a ball flying in the air.
All these different sports helped mold me into
the tight end I am today, with the success I
have today."

Here are just a few ways in which playing
multiple sports can help you develop as an overall
athlete mentally and physically:

- Reduces your risk of injury to certain
  muscles being overworked and other
  muscles not getting much use at all
- Develops hand-eye coordination faster
- Able to face adversity in different settings

brought on through athletics
- Develop better skills as an all-around athlete
- Allows athletes the opportunity to build more mental and life skills
- Better equipped to handle and adapt to new and different environments
- Learn to deal with different types of coaches and coaching styles

And much, much more!

Several college coaches look for athletes who are at least dual-sport student-athletes at the high school level. Many other sports help with an athlete's athleticism, read and reaction timing, and overall skill development for the sport they ultimately choose to focus on in the end.

USC Head Lacrosse Coach and Team USA member, Coach Lindsey Munday, who grew up playing soccer, basketball, and lacrosse in high school, has always told young athletes to play other sports.

Top 5 *reasons why Coach Munday advises high school student-athletes to play multiple sports:*
1. It makes you a better athlete
2. It helps you avoid burnout
3. You learn skills that will help in the sport you do choose
4. It challenges you to work on some skills that you may lack

5. It's just fun

Growing up, I played anything and everything available to me. The first sport that I participated in that was part of an organization or program was soccer. And I absolutely loved every minute of it, running around, chasing a ball, taking contact, and continuing my stride, while aiming to score. These are all things that played a major role and helped me succeed as a basketball player, and did wonders for me as an overall athlete. While playing soccer, the cardio built up my endurance and I noticed it even more during the basketball season because I often played full games with no substitution. Not once did I complain about it; I wanted to be out there the entire time anyways. By playing soccer, I made sure I was built for it.

Another thing that I noticed was how I didn't get taped or wear ankle braces at an early age and would easily bounce back from a rolled or sprained ankle. Even still, to this day, I don't get taped regularly and have great ankle stability. Chasing a ball in the grass and field allowed the ground elements to strengthen my ankles on a different level. I learned to take contact from my opponents as well as the ground and continue pushing along. Knowing I could take a bump and continue going played a considerable part in the mental aspect of my game. Being physical was never a problem at all for me.

While doing all of these things, also trying to score and remain on my feet, playing soccer allowed me to fight through obstacles and focus on the task at hand more than anything else. I gained the ability to continue competing while remaining focused no matter what else was going on around me, or even to me at times because you're physically battling others on the soccer field. Soccer also built up my hand-eye coordination in ways that basketball alone would not have. And doing it at such an early age only helped me flourish even more within the game of basketball.

Throughout my years of playing soccer, I even had coaches who helped grow my athletic abilities by playing me in multiple positions, not just during the season but most of the time during each game. From playing defender to striker to goalie, and always given the opportunity to take the ball and try and score if I felt I could make it happen.

Here I am only speaking about how playing soccer translated to so many great positives for me as a basketball player, and most of this is on the physical side of the game. But the reality is, I could make this same argument for playing softball/ baseball, playing tag with my friends, playing football, and anything else I grew up playing with the neighborhood kids. It wasn't only building up my stamina and physicality for being a serious athlete, it also helped me develop an overall sense of confidence in my athletic ability that made me more often, than not, mentally tougher than other kids at a younger age. The more active you are as a young athlete, the better.

CHAPTER 11

Are You Really Working?

Individual Workouts & Player Development

What work are you really putting in? How much work are you putting in on and off the court to make sure you are at your best? Are you aware of the actual differences between going to the gym to work on your game as an individual and just being in the gym but not really being productive? Nowadays, so many young people walk into a gym, take photos of their surroundings or while dribbling a ball, post it, and then WALK OUT. All while claiming to have had a killer workout and to have been on their grind.

A lot of athletes will talk about getting better, might even show up and go through the motions, get a good sweat in, but refuse to truly do the work, be detailed, and put in the effort that it takes to get better. Do NOT be like them! Set yourself apart and be different to get noticed. You need to be intentional about the work you are putting in to make this all happen. Any time you have an opportunity to work on your game as an individual to get better, do that. Ask for help and take criticism. It takes a lot of time, and it's a big commitment to get in extra work outside of practice time.

Practice time is usually geared towards things that will make your team better, and it's used to implement the game plan and strategy for your upcoming season against your opponents. Even though this is the case, when you are detailed and **FOCUSED** on reaching your next level, you can fully take advantage of every rep possible to increase your game as an individual. Don't just go through the motions of the drill knowing that someone right behind you will be coming up next. Don't hide behind others, hoping to get skipped on your next turn. Be ready to step up and go hard. Someone who enjoys the game and takes their goals of reaching the next level seriously takes advantage of any given opportunity.

Whether you have a trainer, player development coach, or you put in a lot of work on your own, there is always plenty of work to put in towards your personal growth as an athlete. But the question will always be, "what work are you actually putting in?" It is important to compete with the athlete you were the day prior, each and every day.

If you have a trainer, are you making sure they are qualified to get you to the next level? Do they know their stuff, have any credentials, do they have you doing things that can translate to the game and make you a better athlete? Make sure you do your research; I know you have now seen me say that a lot at this point. The same goes for a player development coach, do your research. And if you are going to the gym by yourself to work on your game, that is certainly fine, but are you being intentional about the work you are putting in? Or are you just going through the motions and seeing what happens?

"Athletes please stop doing all these crazy drills that don't apply to your game. A trainer or coach should be able to show you how this translates to your game. If he or she can't, stop the madness now."

"- Deion Sanders via Twitter"

Let me explain further what it means to be intentional with your individual workouts. If you have a personal trainer or a player development coach, this individual should have a plan in place for you before you get to the gym as to what you all will be working on to get better. But if you are working on things by yourself, you should have your own plan of action. If you consider yourself a shooter in the sport of basketball, before you go to the gym make a shooting chart, that way you can track how many shots you take and how many you make. You want to be sure to go to the gym with a purpose. This is how you keep track of whether, or not you are getting better, because you have goals in mind that you are trying to accomplish.

How many shots are you getting up on average? How many of those shots are you making? These are questions you should be able to answer, and if you can't, this is an even more important step for you to take during this process. During my years in high school, I had the personal goal of putting up 200-300 shots daily. I would make my shooting chart, and before I could play pick-up with the guys, I tried to get these shots up on a court nobody was using. I made myself go game speed to resemble the shots I would take during the game; this was also my "warm-up" before playing pick-up.

Ironically, I didn't even consider myself a shooter while in high school and barely took any 3-pointers until my Senior year. I knew that I wanted to expand my game and add to the ways that I could score the basketball, so this was just a part of it for me. My biggest motivator for working on my shot was who I played pick-up against. As a little girl who was about 5'3" when I started playing heavy with the guys, like adult men and not just the boys around my age, I just knew that it wouldn't be smart to continue trying to get layups on men who were 6 feet or above. I got tired of getting blocked or taking certain bumps, so I developed some range in my game.

First, it was the pull-up jumper from mid-range, and then I moved further and further back to the 3pt line and beyond. Shout out to my guy "Big Chuck" who never let me have it easy growing up!

Plus, I had a couple of younger teammates, Haley Klingelhoefer and Courtney and Katie Bergheger, who I considered great shooters at the high school level. I would be in awe of their form and accuracy. They motivated me to step my game up as well. Sometimes I had a rebounder, and other times I didn't, but that didn't stop me from getting my shots up to reach my personal daily goal. I wasn't introduced to a mechanical shooting gun until my Junior year of college when I transferred to the University of Illinois from Rend Lake College. And by that time, I had already increased the number of shots I was getting up daily. Whatever it took to get up 500+ makes a day was what I did. It wasn't about just getting up shots any more, I became more detailed, disciplined, and obsessed with seeing my results. With the introduction of the shooting gun and being around even better shooters, of course, I had to step my game up as well and put in even more work!

It is important to continuously put work in towards your game and to evolve as a player. Be sure to workout with other players, preferably those who are better than you and will push you. Take constructive criticism from those that are trying to help. Take notes and pay attention to how well you are doing; keep track of your progress by using charts. And lastly, work on the details of YOUR game so that you will be able to become the best player you can be.

CHAPTER 12

Social Media
Make It Work For You

Ok people, it's 2021, and if you didn't know just how important social media is these days, luckily, I'm here to tell you! People all over the world have been making their dreams come true by using social media to their advantage. Plenty of opportunities to play at the next level have been given to athletes who used their social media the right way to promote themselves. There are so many positives and negatives that come along with using social media, but are you aware of what those positives and negatives are?

If you use social media the right way, as far as keeping your goals in mind, several doors and opportunities could come your way too. But if you aren't careful or aware and use it the wrong way, opportunities could be lost before you even knew you had them to begin with, so choose your content wisely!

Not only do coaches use it, but also the administration from some colleges and universities have been known to use social media to help make their choices on whether, or not an athlete would be a good fit for their program and institution. When you become a college athlete, you represent so much more than just yourself. You represent a long-standing history for their program, for their school, the community that surrounds it, and of course, your own family, friends, and the community from which you come from.

Being a college athlete is about much more than just being a part of the team and physically playing the game. This is just one reason why it is so important to fully understand your ultimate goal and why you want to play at the next level. This is also why it is so important to do your own research and understand a school's history and reputation in and outside of their athletics program. You need to understand the things you are truly getting yourself into and all that will be required of you when you become a student-athlete at the next level. Fully do your research and gain knowledge about all the things that embody a student-athlete at these schools you have an interest in. Your responsibilities and expectations may not be the same everywhere you go. You could have more, or you could have less, but at the end of the day, you need to at least have an idea.

If you are serious in your pursuit to get to the

next level, almost everything you do should reflect that. Especially your social media. Use it to your advantage and showcase yourself, from your playing abilities to your interests and personality. Social media is a walking billboard for all the things you would like to advertise about yourself.

Coach David Caputo (Head Women's Basketball Coach at Delaware State University) gave out some great insight on how student-athletes on social media could use their accounts to help them get recruited. The first thing you should do as a student-athlete is use your first and last name on all your social media accounts. If you're hoping to get noticed and you've been using your social media already, you don't want to use a profile name that reflects negatively on you. Second, pin your highlights to your profiles, or have the highlights as a "pinned" tweet. Make sure that your highlights are easily accessible. Third, you'll want to have full games and your transcripts ready. You can't be accepted to a school based solely on your highlights; make sure to get those grades ready to be shown. Next, post your NCAA Eligibility Center number. And last but not least, keep your page clean and somewhat professional.

I understand that most people want to post whatever they want, whenever they want, without giving it a second thought. But if you are serious and actively trying to get to your next level, you should shift your focus and use all the tools that are available to you to do so. Besides, those that make it to the next level are not like everyone else. Be aware of what you're posting and how others will perceive it. When you finally reach that next level and join a team, you will be representing a whole new community of people and so much more than yourself. Thinking about that now will show coaches you already know and understand what would be expected of you at the next level and can handle that responsibility. You were proving it before you received their attention, and THAT may be one of the reasons behind you getting your first look and opportunity to the next level! Understand that being a part of that next level is about more than just the sport itself.

Let's talk about some positive ways you can use your social media to your advantage as a student-athlete trying to get to the next level.

1.   FOLLOW coaches on their social media platforms.

Most coaches have social media platforms and those who don't are a little behind on some things. Instagram and Twitter are the platforms where most of these coaches remain active. Coaches are always sharing information about the program they are currently coaching, tips for recruits, tips for other coaches, and sharing some of their personal views about sports and other things. It's very easy to hit that "like" button or to share the things that these coaches post and retweet. Make small comments by leaving an eye-catching question to initiate an interaction. Depending on what you say, you might even get a response back, but don't get discouraged if you don't get one right away. Them not responding right away doesn't mean they didn't see the interaction. By interacting with them on their social media, this will more than likely draw them back to your page or profile. If they don't respond back initially, don't worry about that part too much. You just want to try and get their attention so that they look at your profile and get an idea of who you are.

2.   Make sure your social media is "family-friendly."

It is a bit of an introduction to who you are as a person, so it's completely ok not to have your social media flooded with sports and a "LOOK AT ME I CAN HOOP" billboard. Showcase yourself with your family and friends, show your hobbies and interests outside of athletics. Who knows, you and that coach could have a few things in common or some similarities outside of sports that could draw them into wanting to get to know you better.

3.   Post highlights from some of your games, as well as a few of your workouts.

Posting highlights is a must if you are trying to get noticed. Coaches need to see something from you that shows your capabilities on the court or the field. When you don't already have eyes on you and aren't highly recruited, this is a

108

major way to market yourself and get yourself out there. The more videos you post consistently, the better. And if a coach can see progression in your abilities through the videos you post, that works even more in your favor!

4. Tag coaches in your posts.

If you have already been doing what was stated for #1, then it should be easier to find and tag a couple of coaches on a post regularly. Don't be shy! Getting over the hurdle of putting yourself out there is half of the battle, but be confident behind the posts you are making and go ahead and tag a few coaches so that they can get the first glance.

5. Direct message coaches.

Introduce yourself, ask for a follow, let them know you are interested in reaching the next level and possibly playing for them one day. Ask them for some advice that could help you get to the next level and meet them someday. Just like when it comes to tagging coaches in your posts, don't be shy about sending them a message. Be confident, send a short message, and let the cards fall where they may.

If you are an athlete looking for an opportunity and have not been recruited by many coaches, don't limit yourself to the number of coaches to whom you contact and reach out to. Send out as many messages a day as you can.

Most programs have two or more coaches, and at the Division I level, there are usually four different coaches you can reach. There is always a Head Coach, possibly an Associate Head Coach, and then there is usually an Assistant Coach, maybe even two. Also look for a Strength and Conditioning Coach, or a Player Development Coach. These are all positions that make up a basketball staff at the top levels. The names may change, however, they are still coaches for you to get a hold of. You are trying to reach out to as many people and coaches as you can until you get that opportunity to play at the next level.

6. Give props!

Another way to use your social media to your advantage is to give props where props are due. Any time you hold a conversation with a coach or a school reaches out to you, and things are left on a positive note, shout that coach and that school out on social media. They love positive feedback coming from just about anywhere, and a lot of other coaches and programs become more interested in a player when they see that other coaches and schools are already interested. Is this a weird concept? Possibly, but a lot of times, this is exactly how it works. Coaches are competing during the recruiting period, and they are trying to find the best athletes and fits for their program. Once they see another coach has eyes on an athlete, it piques their interest. They want to know more about the athlete; therefore, they could contact you directly or look through your profile for some game film. For the athlete that isn't highly recruited, this is an excellent opportunity to get that ball rolling. It can work in your favor in more ways than one.

Now, here are some negatives about social media that may disrupt your recruiting process and chances if you are not aware and careful:

1. Derogatory content and prejudice remarks

Paying attention to this type of content is more important now than it's ever been. If you are posting ANYTHING disrespectful and distasteful, especially racially insensitive or prejudice, coaches take this into account. Remember, they are looking at you as a possible prospect and representative of their program. This says a lot about someone's character and what they stand for.

2. Profanity

You may not view this as an issue, but it can be. If you are still in high school, you are considered a young adult. And seeing a bunch of young people post curse words while trying to get into an established institution is never really a good look. I understand that you might be quoting a hot song in your caption but be smart about it. Also, when you are posting your highlight tapes, remember to use an edited song or just use instrumentals. Coaches more than likely have your videos on mute most of the time because it's not about what they are hearing, but what they are seeing. They are more concerned with how you look in the video rather than the sound that's coming out of the speakers.

3. Abusive Language and Posts

Very similar to **derogatory content and profanity,** this portion has slightly different undertones to it. Countless prospects have lost opportunities with certain coaches and schools because of things they have posted and possibly didn't recognize as detrimental. Those words or that post affected others negatively, but even more so, affected the athlete's future tremendously.

4. Nudity

I think this one is pretty self-explanatory, but if you still need help understanding, do not post yourself naked anywhere. Having a student-athlete that has an Only Fans account is not something that most programs and coaches want to deal with. You want to be seen as a role model at the next level, and this is just not age-appropriate for those that look up to you.

5. Drugs and Alcohol

More than likely, you are underage, so there shouldn't be anything out there showing you doing anything illegal pertaining to drugs and alcohol. And even if you are over 21, (age requirements to play college sports differ depending on division and circumstance, i.e. military reserves or veterans) playing at the college level, you have to understand the policies in place that are against drugs or alcohol, so it's better not to have any posts showing you taking part of these activities. Plus, if you are working on being the best athlete you can be, these should be the last things you are thinking about and participating in. Stay away from drugs kids!

"Recruits: social media matters. I have now dropped 15 recruits this year because of their twitter posts, likes, or retweets. Explicit images, racist words, and demeaning posts are unacceptable. Your thumbs are killing your opportunities."

— Coach Joshua Lawson, DI Football Coach at Arkansas Tech via Twitter

CHAPTER 13

Hit The Books!

The most **IMPORTANT** step of them all is to make sure you are hitting the books! If you want to make sure you have the best chance of playing anywhere, if you want to make sure you have as many choices in where you can play, or if you want the opportunity to have as many scholarship options as possible, **MAKE SURE YOUR GRADES ARE ON POINT!!!!**

It's a bit hard to reach the next level and play college sports if you don't get into college. There used to be such a misconception that your grades didn't matter much in high school if you were trying to get an athletic scholarship. I have no idea where that came from, but I've seen so many athletes lose out on opportunities because they didn't take care of business the way they should have. TRUST ME, I KNOW! Even I had this idea in my head at one point during my high school years. The higher your grades are, the more opportunities and options that can come your way. Never lose sight of the "student" in student-athlete.

Everyone has their reasons for wanting to play at the college level, and they aren't all the same. Sometimes that reason is because they hope to receive a free education while also continuing their athletic journey. Maybe your dream school has nothing to do with the athletics' program and everything to do with the major you hope to study, and that's really your driving force behind getting to the next level. Regardless of why you want to play at the next level, if you have the best grades possible, you may be able to choose the school of your dreams much sooner. Instead of receiving an athletic scholarship, you could receive an academic scholarship that gets you in the school and on the team!

Don't you want to make sure you have the best chances of playing somewhere if you can help it? This is part of being proactive in your pursuit of making it to the next level. College coaches usually begin gathering information about you without you even knowing it. They can and will begin contacting your school, your current coach, your AAU coach, and they will most certainly ask about your grades. That door of opportunity for you to reach the next level could close before you even knew it was open if you do not take care of your grades.

Coaches relay messages to one another and talk about the players they were or are recruiting. You could potentially be losing out in abundance due to something you had control over. The better your grades are, the wider that door of opportunity becomes. Coaches from all divisions and levels will reach out to you, but to make sure you have the BEST choices as to where you can play, you want to try and have the highest grade point average possible.

Certain schools, conferences, and divisions have restrictions on who they can accept depending on your GPA. The rules change from time to time, but if you want to be eligible for every possibility out there, a 3.25 is something to strive for. This GPA will allow all schools to consider you, even those in the Ivy League. Anything below that, and you would not qualify for schools like Princeton, Harvard, and Brown. It doesn't matter that you are on an athletic scholarship and not an academic, some institutions have different qualifications, and some require stricter qualifications than others.

The minimum GPA needed for a student-athlete to still be NCAA eligible for Division I athletics is 2.3. A 900 SAT or 75 ACT sum score is also required on top of that for Division I. At the Division II level, a 2.2 GPA and 840 SAT or 70 ACT sum is needed. In the end, the minimum GPA is dependent upon where you fall on the NCAA sliding scale.

www.ncsasports.org/ncaa-eligibility-center/ncaa-sliding-scale

"The NCAA does not use the GPA listed on

117

your transcripts; instead, it calculates your GPA using only NCAA-approved core courses."

www.ncsasports.org/ncaa-eligilibilty-center/gpa-requirements

The number of student-athletes deemed academically ineligible because they took the wrong courses and just didn't know it until it was too late is unimaginable. Simply because this can be prevented. The student-athlete may have the overall minimum GPA, but without knowing this bit of information about making sure that they have been taking NCAA-approved courses, they could find out about their ineligibility after the fact.

Be sure to schedule meetings with your guidance counselor several times throughout each school year to make sure you stay on track. Ask for a checklist of requirements and tasks that are needed to be accomplished before graduation. Do whatever it takes to make sure you have taken all the classes needed to graduate, the classes required to have the best GPA you can have, and the courses that will give you the best chances to get you into the institutions you hope to attend.

You are giving yourself the opportunity to receive as many scholarship options and ways to make it to the next level as possible. This thought should always include an academic scholarship.

Coaches are ALWAYS looking for players for their program, and what they are looking for ranges in many ways. The information I'm sharing is something that coaches may not tell you, but I'm here to give you some insight on what these programs are looking for and what you can do to make sure you are someone they could potentially be looking for and need on their team! With a great GPA, many coaches would love to have you as a part of their program. There are times when coaches may not be able to offer you an athletic scholarship because they used their allotted amount, but if you have a high enough GPA that reaches the requirements of the school, that coach could be able to have you as a part of their program on an academic scholarship instead. To ensure that you qualify for this opportunity and have it as an option, you need to make sure you do the work early and hit the books while in high school! Remember, YOU are just looking for a foot in the right door, so you can get the opportunity to play at the next level! What you do with the opportunity is up to you.

CHAPTER 14

What Do College Coaches Look For?

C ollege coaches are different people with different plans for their programs. Just like you have your goals, coaches have theirs as well. Every coach is NOT looking for the same thing in all of their players, and from the players they recruit. They don't have the same goals all the way across the board, just like you as an athlete do not have the same goals as every other athlete you may run into. This is an essential factor to remember in your journey.

This is another reason it is important to know what you are looking for as an athlete trying to reach your next level, and why networking and building a relationship with coaches is critical as well. Make sure to search for the type of coach and program that best suits you and your needs as not only an athlete, but also as a person. You should be looking for a coach that can best help you reach your goals and help you grow along the way. Although every coach may not need or be looking for the same things from every player, there are a few things that you can count on that all coaches are indeed happy to have as part of their program.

Every coach could certainly use a player that brings in additional value to their team and program, but what does that look like coming from you?

When speaking with coaches, make it a point to ask them specifically what they are looking for in a player? If you have already developed a relationship with this coach, they are recruiting you, and they have seen you play before, ask them what they would be expecting from you if you become a part of their team?

If you are a guard, you'll want to know what you need to work on and get better at to fit their program and so many others. That coach could tell you, "I am looking for a 2 guard who can not only shoot the ball pretty well, but play defense on one of the opponent's best players, and to sometimes bring the ball up the floor to give our point guard some relief from time to time." From that statement alone, you have learned that if you have subpar defensive skills, then that is something that you need to work on. You will also need to get up more shots and work on pushing the ball up the floor or taking reps with point guards to understand how to run the offense from that spot. There's plenty of feedback within that statement and that encounter with a coach that you could run with and begin bettering your game to help their program, and many others in the process. That's just one example.

CHAPTER 15

What Does YOUR Opportunity Look Like?

As you enter this journey, please understand that it's a marathon and not a sprint. Your journey and path through athletics and reaching the next level will always be unique, despite what others have done or gone through. Do not base your path off the perception you have of others. Rarely do we get the full glimpse into the exact roadmap of an athlete. There are conversations, options, and recommendations given to different athletes, at different times, for different reasons. These interactions often lead to different types of opportunities, but will you recognize yours when it comes if it does not look like the average?

As long as you keep your ultimate goal in mind and hold yourself accountable for the work you are or aren't putting in, you will know when it is necessary for you to accept, make moves, or to stay put. I wrote this book to help you understand your goals and realize the amount of work it might take to get there. All you need is that one opportunity to get you in the door and hopefully you'll be willing to continue to work hard and make things happen from there! Your first opportunity might require you to have very humble beginnings, you may not have a scholarship at first, might not be in the division of dreams to start, or what if you have to start out by being a manager?

"Turning down an offer because it's not D1 and you don't have any other offers is a lot like turning down a really good paying job with great benefits and growth potential simply because you think you should be hired as the VP of the company with no experience!"

- Coach William Payne via Twitter

Walk On

When looking for an opportunity to play at the next level, there are several different options to consider; becoming a "walk-on" for that coach at that college or university is one of them. When coaches see potential in a player and don't have any scholarships to offer them, they can offer a "walk-on" spot instead, in most cases. This option is more so offered to a player that may live close by, but it can be offered to any athlete, no matter where they reside. This allows a player to still be a part

126

of the team, to grow and learn about the program, and to possibly keep their eligibility if they do not play in a game all season.

It's one thing for a coach to offer this as an option to an athlete, but when an athlete offers to take on this option on their own it says a lot about how hard that athlete is willing to work to prove themselves worthy of being on that team and playing at the next level.

Offering to be a "walk-on" shows that you just want an opportunity and you are willing to earn it through hard work and dedication. You are letting the coach know that they have nothing to lose and everything to gain by allowing you the opportunity to be a part of the team and to earn a spot. You are willing to work for it and sacrifice right away. This says a lot about an athlete, but even more about their character when they have limited options.

Go into it with the mindset of working your way up in hopes of gaining a scholarship. This is not always the easiest or affordable option, but it IS an option. Think about the things you are willing to sacrifice and work for to get your opportunity to play at the next level. Your effort, commitment, and dedication could lead to a scholarship for the following season or even for the second semester. Taking on the role as a "walk-on" is a lot of hard work and is not an easy task. Not everyone is capable of being in that humbling position. If you are considering this option, have conversations with the coaches about this possibility ***EARLY!*** It allows you the opportunity to be a part of summer workouts and anything else the team may have going on. It also puts you on the roster before someone else comes along with the same idea.

During my time as the head coach at Rend Lake College, I awarded scholarships to walk-ons who consistently showed a lot of hard work and dedication throughout the first semester and preseason workouts. They led by example and proved they were indeed deserving of a scholarship, and since I had a couple of scholarships available, I made sure they received one for the second semester. There was a player who made straight A's, never missed a practice, never was late, and was working themselves back from an injury that ended their high school career a little earlier than expected.

She had a lot of heart and showed up every day without question. She was also working a part-time job and showed a level of maturity and discipline that everyone else just did not quite have as freshmen and sophomores. She was not afraid to be coached, and she also took the initiative in finding time outside of practice to get more work in. These are the types of players that coaches always enjoy and are looking to extend a helping hand to, so giving them a scholarship they have rightfully earned is not hard at all.

If you are considering the option of being a "walk-on," first and foremost, you NEED to make sure that your grades won't be an issue. You want to make sure that this is NOT something that coaches at the next level need to be concerned about when it comes to you. By making sure that your grades are together, this is already something of value that you are telling coaches you will bring to their team and program. With the addition of you to their team roster, you should at the very least be able to hold the team's GPA to a certain standard. Coaches appreciate and value a player who has this quality, shows great work ethic on and off the court.

Prep School

Getting into a prep school is also another option. This is a unique option, but it isn't for everybody. These institutions are there to help guide you and prepare you for the next level as well. But the guidelines to get into these institutions differ across the board. Across the nation, several can be found and are pretty well known, but then there are a few that are not so well known, mostly because of their selection process. Prep schools can be considered "next level" as is. Some of these institutions give out scholarships for athletes to attend as high school athletes or during a preparation year that comes right after high school.

They are there to help bridge the gap between high school athletics and collegiate/professional athletics. Prep schools allow the athletes to hone skills as a student and as a student- athlete. It is more of an accelerated program than most. You are there with one focus in mind, and that is to be better! In all facets!

CHAPTER 16

Should I Redshirt?

Another way of getting the most out of your athletic career in college is to lengthen your period of eligibility by becoming a "redshirt" if you were to receive that option. Now, with the option of becoming a "redshirt," which usually takes place during your freshman year, it gives you five years of academics but four years of athletics. You're ultimately part of the team and get all the perks as a team member, except you can't play in games during this "redshirt" year. This is the most popular option amongst those athletes afforded this opportunity, however, there are other "shirts" available. They are just a bit less talked about and utilized more within other sports. Let's talk about all the different types of shirts so you can understand them and see if any of these options would be available to you.

Redshirt

Like I mentioned before, being a "redshirt" for a program is the most common shirt type. You are given a scholarship, and you can practice with the team, but you cannot suit up and play in games. You also get to keep that year of eligibility. Most people who consider this option take this during their freshman year, which allows them 4 years of eligibility as an athlete playing in NCAA competition, and they spend a year getting acclimated with the program and the institution.

Greenshirt

As a "greenshirt," you enroll in college a whole semester early. There's a scholarship for you in place already and when the season begins you can both play in games and practice with the team. More than likely, with this option, you were already heavily recruited and they wanted you on campus as soon as possible. Also, you were probably in a great position to graduate from high school early allowing this option to take place.

Blueshirt

With the "blueshirt" option, you may not have been formally recruited, but still received an opportunity. The school year may have already started when a coach reached out to you, and you were offered and given a scholarship. In this situation, you may have already been attending this college and the coach noticed your abilities and reached out. Due to the circumstances and timing, you can only practice with the team and cannot play in games this season. But more than likely you have now committed to playing for this coach next season.

Grayshirt

If you go the "grayshirt" route, you do not have a scholarship and cannot practice or play in games. But all is not lost; you have to wait an extra semester before becoming a full-time student and a part of the team. That does not mean that you don't have access to the gym, the players, the coaching staff and can't work out or develop chemistry with your teammates. You just can't participate in the things that are organized and structured for the team under certain guidelines.

Knowing the different types of SHIRTS you can be and still be a part of a college program is important! You just being aware and educated about the different options may present the opportunity you have been working towards.

CHAPTER 17

What To Do While Being Recruited

As mentioned earlier in this book, once coaches begin communicating with you regularly, it's time to really get the ball rolling. Make sure you continue to ask questions and pick their brains to see if their program and institution will be the right fit for you. It's important to keep the lines of communication open and really get a feel for all the things you want out of a program and coach.

Here are just a few questions that you should ask coaches during the recruiting process:

- 1. Which coach on staff will oversee my player development?
- 2. Will there be a summer workout program?
- 3. Would I have to do summer school and be on campus during the summer? Is that option available?
- 4. Are there any majors that I cannot pursue as a student-athlete at your school?

- *5. What type of skills or skill-set are you looking for in players that play my position?*

After having any real interaction with a coach or program, whether that be a phone call or in-person, you should acknowledge this interaction over social media. This simple act of acknowledgment goes a long way with the program itself, but also for your personal recruitment. What tends to happen is that other schools, athletes, and coaches take note of who is starting to recruit you. This, in turn brings more "traffic" to your efforts to get recognized so you can get to the next level, which was the goal in the first place!

Now...understand this, if you have gotten all your questions answered by a school or coach, you have been on a visit to this school, and the school has OFFERED you a scholarship, if the school checks all the boxes for you, this might be the school for you. What some athletes do, is they make the mistake of taking too long to make the decision when they have the answer in front of them, thinking that they will miss out on the next best thing. They get caught up in waiting for the next best opportunity to come through, and for an athlete who may have had NO recruitment happening beforehand, this is a mistake that you can avoid. Unfortunately, if you take too long to accept the offer, then that school could move on and offer the scholarship to another athlete.

Outside of weighing options and posting bits of the recruiting process while going through it, do not stop doing the things that got you to this point. Continue to do your workouts, study the game, get better, and hit the books. Now is not the time to get lax and feel like you have "made it." It's time to double down on your efforts!

CHAPTER 18

Can You Handle Your Role?

A lot of times, the players that are highly recruited go into their next level with the assumption that they will come into a situation and be the "star" player or average 30 min and be a starter. On the other hand, the athletes that aren't as highly recruited enter the situation with a mentality of being ready to work and earn a spot, simply because they took a different route to receive their opportunity. So many athletes have set themselves up for failure or disappointment by having a view of entitlement and expectations. Ask yourself if you are willing to earn your spot and play your role? Are you able to play a role or position that you aren't used to so that you have an opportunity at the next level?

You need to know whether, or not you can handle playing different roles than what you are accustomed to. This could be considered a major sacrifice to continue your playing career. There have been plenty of athletes who have made careers out of being a great role player and doing everything they could to help their team win at the next level. There are also plenty of athletes who have floundered and decimated their journeys because they were unable to embrace a new role.

When reaching the next level you may not be the best on the team, but are you the type of player who is the best for that team? If you are, then coaches will find it hard to turn you down. There have been many great role players to make it to the highest level. These players were seen as stars in high school, or even college, but their next levels required a different part of their game as their focus. These people became the players that would do all the little things and more. Coaches enjoy players who can accept a role, handle it with grace, and do it to the best of their ability, no matter what may be asked of them. Having this type of mentality creates roles and positions that may not have been available before, because sometimes the things that matter the most for that team, program, or coach, are things that don't necessarily show up on a stat sheet.

"Do you want to be an uncommon player?
Box out, take charges, dive for loose balls, and
make the extra pass. Those are all things that
everyone can do but yet, few actually do them."

– Jeff Van Gundy

As a sophomore in high school, Michael Jordan didn't make the varsity team and was cut. Steve Kerr didn't have any offers coming out of high school. Dennis Rodman went from a JUCO to an NAIA school. Scottie Pippen had to walk on at an NAIA to get his first opportunity. What do all these players have in common? Their paths were all different and it took overcoming some adversity before they got together as professionals. And once they got there, each of their roles were a bit different than what their roles were at earlier pit stops in their journey. Take advantage of the opportunities that are in front of you and as they come, and then use them to accomplish your goals.

CHAPTER 19

Conclusion

Now that you have a blueprint, a list of coaches, a list of schools, and have placed priority on the things you would like to accomplish through your journey within sports, the real fun begins. Embrace the journey, tackle things head on, and no longer sit back waiting for things to come to you. The game continuously evolves on and off the court, and you should too. You have more things working in your favor today as a young athlete than anyone ever has, it's time you took full advantage of it.

Have you made your first move yet? Have you reached out to coaches? Have you made any posts? Told people about your dreams? The hardest part has always been about making the first move and being fully committed to putting yourself out there. You are more than capable of accomplishing all the goals you have set for yourself.

Now that we have come to the end of this book I

hope that I have motivated you to go after all that you hope to accomplish, not just within athletics but in life. Put a plan together and start acting on it. Make decisions today that will help you get further in the future. You may hear the word "no" a time or two but do not let that stop you. That just means you have not found your opportunity yet and that you need to continue putting in more work, but you're mentally prepared to do so now more than ever.

About The Author

Rebecca T. Harris is the daughter of Johnnie and Belynda Harris. The 2nd oldest of 4, born on March Air Force Base in California, Rebecca and her siblings (Jay Omar, Beryl & Jasmyne) grew up living abroad most of their lives while their father served in the United States Air Force. From growing up, living overseas, to becoming a professional basketball player, her journey would have her play multiple seasons abroad. Even still, until this day, she has dedicated most of her time and energy outside of playing basketball, to sharing her experiences to help those who try and accomplish their goals.

She has earned a bachelor's degree in Communications from the University of Illinois, where she was also a Division I basketball player, but not before becoming an honorable JUCO All-American while attending and playing at Rend Lake College. There she is forever etched in the record books as a Hall of Famer.

Since graduating from the University of Illinois in 2008, she has played several seasons overseas in such countries as Greece, Czech Republic, Poland, Turkey, Germany, and the Ukraine. Throughout her playing career,

Rebecca did take opportunities to step away and coach at the high school and college levels, being an assistant at Chipola College (2012- 2013), head coach at Mascoutah High School (2016-2017), and Rend Lake College (2017-2018). During the off seasons from playing across the country, Rebecca can be found training and working out with young student-athletes in the Midwest areas of Illinois and Missouri, while also playing in a summer season with the St. Louis Surge.

For more about Rebecca Harris, please visit Rebecca30Harris.com.

Acknowledgements

It's certainly true what they say about this being the hardest part of the book to write. Let's be real, I couldn't have possibly made it this far in life and this journey without those that prayed for me, encouraged me, challenged me, walked beside me, or even left me high and dry. Life has been full of lessons and ups along with downs. I am grateful for all of it.

Thank you to my parents, Johnnie and Belynda, for seeing something inside me and providing me with opportunities to flourish. There aren't enough words to describe how grateful I am for the life you provided and the places you made sure I was able to see at a young age. Ultimately shaping the way I viewed the world and its' endless opportunities. That might have been one of the most significant gifts of my life. I love you both dearly.

To my brother Josh (JayOmar Scott Harris) and my sisters, Beryl and Jasmyne, thank you for the sacrifices you all made. Thank you for the fun times and adventures. Thank you for the cheers and encouragement throughout my lifetime and please continue. Thank you for being constants in this journey. I love you!

To my many coaches over the years, there's no doubt that you have each taught me some life lessons that I will continue to cherish for the rest of my days. Coach Moeller, Coach Box, Coach Law, Coach Edo, Coach Franklin, Coach Grentz, Coach Frese, and Coach Mode (RIP), you all are just a few of the names to leave a lasting imprint on my life. I can't thank you enough for teaching me so much about the game of basketball and the game of life, on and off the court.

To the many young athletes that come to me in search of some answers and direction based on my personal experiences, I hope I've done right by you. I will continue to provide you with the tools and information as long as I can. Because of you and my own story, I want to continue to be that person for you because I know what it's like not to have that person while I was coming up. This is for you.

To my friends, my circle of people closest to me, I appreciate you! The ones that always encourage me and keep me grounded, I thank you. Living a life of traveling back and forth abroad while life continues to take place on the other side of the world can be a lonely place at times, but you've always been there.

Last but certainly not least...My heart, partner in crime, fellow globetrotter, and teammate in life...Kristi I could not have finished this and put it together without you! Thank you for everything you do and everything you are to me!

Made in the USA
Coppell, TX
09 September 2022

82875779R00083